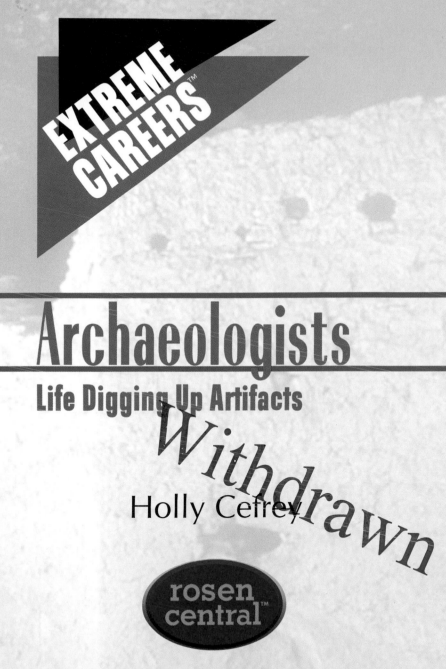

EXTREME CAREERS™

Archaeologists
Life Digging Up Artifacts

Withdrawn

Holly Cefrey

rosen central™

The Rosen Publishing Group, Inc., New York

Published in 2004 by The Rosen Publishing Group, Inc.
29 East 21st Street, New York, NY 10010

First Edition

Library of Congress Cataloging-in-Publication Data

Cefrey, Holly.
Archaeologists : life digging up artifacts / by Holly Cefrey.
    p. cm. — (Extreme careers)
Summary: Examines the careers available in the field of archaeology, discussing the necessary education, training, and on-the-job duties.
Includes bibliographical references and index.
ISBN 0-8239-3963-4 (lib. bdg.)
1. Archaeologists—Juvenile literature. 2. Archaeology—Juvenile literature.
[1. Archaeology—Vocational guidance. 2. Vocational guidance.] I.
Title. II. Series.
CC107.C44 2003
930.1'023—dc21

                                                        2002153686

Manufactured in the United States of America

Contents

Introduction: Bone Hunting

When you think about an archaeologist, perhaps Indiana Jones comes to mind. He is the fictional character in George Lucas and Steven Spielberg's archaeological adventure movies. Indiana dodges giant rolling boulders, dupes treasure-crazy Nazis, and escapes an ancient snake-filled tomb. During his downtime, he is a university professor.

If you were to compare Indiana's tales to a real archaeologist's life, you would see big differences. Most archaeologists never get to fight evil enemies. Most never dodge giant rolling boulders or ride runaway mining carts. Most archaeologists will not experience any of the death-defying adventures that Indiana has.

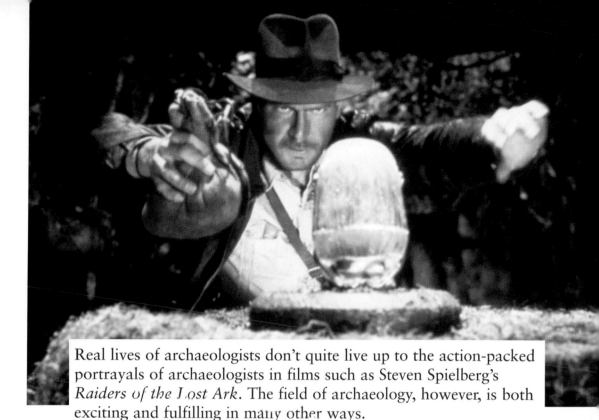

Real lives of archaeologists don't quite live up to the action-packed portrayals of archaeologists in films such as Steven Spielberg's *Raiders of the Lost Ark*. The field of archaeology, however, is both exciting and fulfilling in many other ways.

There are some truths to Indiana's archaeological tales. Archaeologists do go in search of artifacts (ancient objects). Archaeologists also travel to exotic foreign lands. They research mysterious cultures and learn ancient languages. Many archaeologists teach at universities when they are not in search of artifacts. Many archaeologists also get an opportunity to experience a once-in-a-lifetime find or discovery.

Archaeology may not be action-packed, but it is still extreme. One discovery can lead to years of

Archaeologists: Life Digging Up Artifacts

intense work in the field and laboratory. It takes dedication to be a good archaeologist. Every artifact must be carefully observed, studied, and documented. The archaeologist imagines what the artifact was used for and who used it.

Some archaeologists do face risks while at work. There are hazards in the field and in the lab. Some digs are in deep, dark caves. The archaeologist has to rope or climb down hundreds of feet. One wrong step at a dig, and a piece of history can be ruined underfoot.

Archaeologists often find themselves digging in caves beneath the earth to discover artifacts from long ago. Caution and care are needed. Archaeologists want to discover items safely and bring them unharmed to the outside world.

Some substances found at dig sites can be poisonous or harmful to humans. These substances include molds, fungi, and germs. Sometimes weather conditions can quickly turn severe. Sharp, broken, and heavy artifacts must also be handled carefully. They can cause injury. At the lab, chemicals may be used to clean the artifacts. These chemicals can cause burns and injuries if not handled properly.

There are risks in underwater archaeology as well. Many underwater sites are at great depths. Being at great depths for long periods of time can be harmful to humans. It can lead to serious health problems. Also, old wreckage may have parts that fall when disturbed. This can trap or injure divers.

While there is risk in archaeology, there is also great reward. A discovery can solve a mystery that is hundreds or thousands of years old. Each discovery also teaches us about our past. Archaeologists examine or study artifacts to tell us how our ancestors lived.

Days of Digging

The summer sun beats down. You wipe the sweat from your forehead. The sound of a pickax hitting rock carries off into the distance. Your team has been at this dig for three months. Each day, it takes an hour by jeep to get to the site. The water that you drink has to be boiled so that you will not get sick. Within the month, you hope to be back at the museum.

You sit back for a moment, jotting notes in your field book. While you take a break, you watch as the twenty members of the team carry out the excavation. Slowly and carefully, layers of dirt are removed. Every inch of the dig is charted or mapped on paper. Objects are studied before they are removed from the ground. Artifacts are drawn, numbered, and photographed. The artifacts are then examined inside a tent—your makeshift laboratory. Then they are carefully packed so that they can be sent to the museum.

You put your field book down and return to your work. You use a fine brush to remove the loose dirt around something that you have found. So far, the team has found animal bones. The bones are thousands of years old. The bones have scratches and marks on them. Your team believes that humans made

Pictured here is a typical archaeological site, or dig. Archaeologists use special tools to uncover and help preserve the clues that will help them re-create the story of the past.

the marks. You hope to find the bones of the humans who you believe lived here long ago.

The piece that you are working on slowly comes loose. It is a small rock, but it is no ordinary rock. It has sharp edges, which were made by humans. You have found an ancient human tool. It may have even been the sharp tool that made marks on the animal bones. Your heart beats with excitement. Now you know that humans were here.

You tell the rest of your team. Everyone is excited. Within the next few weeks, your team discovers many more tools. Human bones are also found. Who were these people? What were they like? Your team has just begun to find out the history of these people of the past.

Imagine being the first person to unearth an ancient city. Imagine finding the bones of an ancient warrior. Imagine solving the five-thousand-year-old mystery of what happened at a place where all the villagers died at once. Archaeologists get to challenge themselves with many thrilling possibilities of the past.

Archaeology (ancient study) is a science. The archaeologist discovers and studies past human cultures or societies. Each group that is studied has its own values, customs, and beliefs. An archaeologist does research about a culture. He or she studies the artifacts from that culture. He or she also tries to find out when and how the culture developed. This study can take an archaeologist to any place on the planet.

Some archaeologists try to solve puzzling issues. They may try to solve mysteries about a culture's ruin or disappearance. They may try to find out why a culture did certain things. They may try to discover why a culture changed dramatically from its origins. For example, an archaeologist would try to find out why a culture that fished developed into a culture that farmed. What caused the culture to stop fishing? What made them start farming? These questions may be answered through archaeology.

You may wonder why it is so important to learn about our human past. It is important because it teaches us about being human. It shows us how creative and resourceful humans really are—and have been. The past is important because it tells us how we became what we are today. It also explains how and why we have so many different cultures. It teaches us to respect those cultures, and our own.

The Past of Digging

Before archaeology became a science, ancient things were treated differently. Artifacts or ancient discoveries were mostly used for show and conversation. They were hardly used for scientific and scholarly purposes. Places where ancient things were found were often carelessly stripped of artifacts, which were sold as art or souvenirs.

During the 1700s, artifacts were actually thrown away or overlooked unless they had financial value. Tomb raiders and treasure hunters cared very little about the history of our past. They cared about the money or prestige that a great find would bring.

Bones of extinct (no longer existing) animals were also discovered in the 1700s. This discovery captured the imagination of scholars. Some bones were found mixed with sharp tools. The tools were simple and made of stone. Scholars wondered about the humans who made the tools. They began to wonder, "How long have we been here?"

Archaeology became more scientific during the 1800s. Scholars began to excavate (dig) sites more carefully. They started looking at all artifacts instead of

An illustration from the eighteenth century depicts European explorers inspecting and taking measurements of the famous statues found on Polynesia's Easter Island.

just valuable treasures. European scholars studied and researched ancient texts, such as the Bible and those of ancient Greek and Roman writers. The texts described ancient cultures of Europe and the Middle East. The texts helped them look for places to start digs. The texts also helped them understand the artifacts that they found.

During the 1900s, scientists found ways to determine the date the artifacts were made. This told

Fast Fact

President Thomas Jefferson was one of the first people in America to use archaeological techniques that are still used today. He was interested in ancient Native American cultures that had lived in Virginia. He carried out a careful dig of a burial mound near his home, Monticello, during the 1780s.

archaeologists when the humans who made them were alive. Now archaeologists knew when a culture existed by the dating of artifacts.

Archaeologists began to write and document their findings during the 1800s and 1900s. This allowed other diggers and archaeologists to read about a dig. They read about what methods were used during a dig. They read about the artifacts and the culture that the original archaeologists were studying.

Studying Humans

Archaeology is actually a branch, or part, of a larger science. The larger science is called anthropology. Anthropology is the study of human beings—past and present. It is the study of what humans are, where we come from, and why we do the things we do.

An archaeologist usually begins his or her career by getting a degree in anthropology. He or she will also study other subjects, such as foreign languages, history, biology, geology, and computer science. An archaeology student has to gain field experience, too. He or she will work on a dig team and learn from the archaeologists and anthropologists at the site.

Anthropology can be divided into four main parts: Cultural anthropology, physical anthropology, linguistic anthropology, and archaeology.

Cultural Anthropology

A cultural anthropologist studies human cultures. A cultural anthropologist may study a tribe that lives in a faraway jungle. He or she studies the culture of this group, including the customs and rituals of its people. The cultural anthropologist may then compare this group to another tribe or culture. The anthropologist finds differences and similarities between the two groups.

Physical Anthropology

A physical anthropologist studies how we developed as living beings throughout time. Scientists believe that modern humans developed from apelike beings. A physical anthropologist may search for and study

Physical anthropologists study the progress of human development, as shown by this collection of skulls. Humans have been linked to apelike creatures, called hominids, which existed long ago.

bones from these beings. He or she figures out whether the bones are from any of our apelike ancestors, or from other beings.

Linguistic Anthropology

A linguistic anthropologist studies the language of a civilization or a society, including the origin,

Pyramids of Wonder

Archaeologists have wondered how the Great Pyramid of Giza was built. Archaeologist Mark Lehner heads a team that seeks to find the answer. His team has uncovered areas where he believes thousands of laborers lived during the pyramid's construction.

The team is also taking part in a National Geographic Society program to explore the Great Pyramid. Inside the Great Pyramid is the Queen's Chamber. The chamber has very complicated shafts. Archaeologists are not sure why the shafts were built. Humans cannot enter certain areas to find out because stones block the way. The program is using a custom-built robot to explore the shafts. The robot has high-resolution cameras and radar. The archaeologists hope to learn more about the Great Pyramid with this technology.

development, and spread of its languages.
For example, he or she may study how a tribe
uses language and how that language has developed over time.

Crossing the Boundaries of Study

An archaeologist may work with anthropologists
from the other branches. For example, when a
strange or unknown artifact is found, an archaeologist may turn to cultural anthropology. He or she
will find a modern culture or society that is similar
or related to the culture that he or she is studying.
The archaeologist may work with a cultural
anthropologist who knows about the modern
culture. Together they will look for similarities
between the two cultures. The purpose of the
artifact may become clear through the comparison.
The modern culture may be using something
similar to the artifact that was found. It may
have also used something similar to the artifact in
its history.

The Mystery of History

Human beings have lived on Earth for more than one million years. Modern humans, however, did not begin to use written words or symbols until around 5,500 years ago.

The time before written words were used is known as prehistory. Because there are no written words or stories from prehistoric times, we do not know exactly what life was like then. When written words were created, it became possible for people to pass their stories to future generations, which became the history of a people.

An archaeologist can find out what life was like in prehistoric and historic times. All that he or she needs are artifacts from that time. Artifacts give clues about a civilization's culture, technology, and behavior. Tools tell us how ancient people hunted, farmed, or made clothes. Pottery explains how people ate or carried water and food from one place to another. Many artifacts are buried beneath layers of soil and earth. Bodies of water cover many artifacts as well. Artifacts may be wherever humans have lived throughout time. The hunt for artifacts is endless.

Excavation Tools

Archaeologists use special tools to dig for artifacts. All of these tools are familiar to other jobs:

- Trowel—A trowel is often used by bricklayers. The trowel is a small, flat, handheld tool. It is used in archaeology to scrape layers of dirt away.
- Brushes—A variety of brushes are used for delicate removal of dirt. Brushes include toothbrushes and paintbrushes.
- Dental picks and tools—Dental tools are used for working on bones and grave deposits.
- Shovels and buckets—Shovels and buckets are used to remove large deposits of soil.
- Pickax—A pickax is used to remove hard rock deposits from archaeological structures. It is used if there is no danger of damaging the artifact.
- Sieve—A sieve is a screen with holes. Small bits of dirt are sifted on the screen. The dirt falls through. Small archaeological bits do not. Archaeological bits may include fish bones and bits of metal.

Telltale Signs

In historic and prehistoric times, humans lived in many different parts of the world. Wherever humans live, they leave things behind. Some of these things may last for hundreds of thousands of years. They may be preserved beneath the changing landscape. When something is preserved, it means that it has been kept safe from spoiling or disappearing.

Think about the things that you throw away. Your trash goes to a dump. Dumps are large deposits of waste. Now imagine that hundreds of years have passed. The dump is covered beneath layers of land and plants.

A future archaeological team will begin a dig right above the dump. The team may find such things as broken computers, sneakers, television sets, and microwave ovens. The archaeologist would examine these things. He or she would begin to picture what life was like during your time. He or she would also do research into historic written accounts of life during your time. This will complete the picture. Archaeologists will learn what your culture was about and who your people were.

Archaeologists are not grossed out by old trash. Ancient trash can show a great deal about a past civilization. Trash deposits from the past are called middens. A midden may contain things that past civilizations threw out. They can contain pottery, tools, rocks, charcoal, and bones.

Pottery designs, shapes, styles, and uses can show things about a civilization. The insides of pots may be tested to learn what was stored in them. Different types of animal bones show what was eaten or used for food. If tools are found, they can tell an archaeologist about

This pile of oyster shells marks an ancient culture's food midden (trash deposit). Middens tell archaeologists about the diet, tool use, clothing, and cooking utensils of past humans.

DANGER ALERT!

A midden can contain organic (natural) waste. Harmful germs can live in this organic waste. An archaeologist has to be careful if germs are present. These germs can cause infection and serious illness. An archaeologist will wear a mask and gloves to prevent the spread of and infection from midden germs.

the civilization, too. If the tools are very simple, then the civilization was probably less advanced than modern cultures. As humans developed, tools became more complex. Thousands of years ago, sharp stones were used to cut things. Sharp knives, scalpels, sawing devices, and lasers are used to cut things now.

Profile of the Archaeologist

Archaeology involves a great deal of thought, curiosity, and imagination. A farm field is a big slab of dirt to an ordinary person. To an archaeologist, it is where early settlers may have once lived. Battles may have been fought there. Prehistoric humans may have roamed there. It is a possible place to begin a dig.

An excavation can turn up many artifacts. The archaeologist has to know exactly how to treat these artifacts. He or she also uses curiosity and imagination to give each artifact a purpose. What was the artifact used for? How was it made? What were the people like who used it? Archaeologists study the artifacts to find answers to these questions.

The physical side of archaeology is important as well. An archaeologist should be in good health. Many sites are located in areas that can only be reached by walking, hiking, and underwater diving. Some routes to digs may even involve sand mounds, steep hills, mountains, and deep, twisting caves.

Field equipment, such as shovels and hand tools, must be carried to and from a site. The excavation of a site may involve long hours and many weeks of physical labor. The archaeologist should be able to stoop, sit, and work for long periods of time.

At very remote or faraway sites, camp may be pitched. Supplies, comforts, and fresh water may be lacking. An archaeologist learns how to live without the comforts of home.

INFECTION ALERT!

According to *National Geographic* magazine, archaeologist Guillermo "Willy" Cock said that he developed an infection in his throat from his experience at a dig. Doctors have not been able to cure the infection. Cock told *National Geographic* that his team experienced several health problems, including skin infections, colds, and flu. The conditions of the village where the site was found may have caused the illness. There was no electricity, sewage system, or fresh water.

His find: A once-in-a lifetime discovery of thousands of Incan mummies. The mummies were put there about 500 years ago. Three excavation seasons were spent at the site from 1999 to 2001. His team found over 2,200 mummies. The mummies were

Susan Haun and Kerby Cock (Guillermo's son) study the Incan mummies outside Lima, Peru.

found in mummy bundles. A mummy bundle contains more than one mummy. About forty of the bundles had artifacts that indicated the people were of high rank in Incan society.

The villagers who now live above the grave believe that the mummies cause illness. Cock told *National Geographic* magazine that his cough was due to bacteria from the mummies.

More than 60,000 objects and artifacts were recovered from the site. The finds will tell archaeologists about the political, social, and economic system of the Incas.

Opening Up the Underwater World

Underwater archaeology began in the 1940s, when Jacques-Yves Cousteau and Émile Gagnan invented the Aqua-Lung. The Aqua-Lung allowed people to breathe while underwater. We know the Aqua-Lung today as scuba (self-contained underwater breathing apparatus) gear.

According to *National Geographic*, anthropologist George Bass used scuba gear to explore ancient Mediterranean shipwrecks in the 1960s. This began archaeological work in the underwater world.

Underwater archaeology helped scientists discover thousands of artifacts perfectly preserved under the sand.

Sites of the Past

Any place that has evidence of past human life is an archaeological site. Sites are discovered in many ways. Natural disasters such as floods can remove layers of soil. This may expose artifacts or evidence of past human life. Building construction may also uncover a site. These things can also ruin a site.

There are government agencies and private businesses that are concerned with saving threatened sites. They employ archaeologists. These archaeologists survey, excavate, and protect sites that may be in danger. This type of archaeological work is called cultural resource management. This type of work employs many archaeologists.

Finding the Past

Sometimes ordinary people can stumble across an archaeological site. For example, on September 12, 1940, four teens found a site in southern France. They were looking for their lost dog named Robot. What they discovered was the entrance to a cave. The cave is named Lascaux Cave. Inside of the cave are ancient paintings. Ancient hunters made the paintings about

Four French teens accidentally found these ancient cave drawings in 1940. Archaeologists later dated the pictures of wild animals to 15,000 years ago.

Ruining the Past

Lascaux Cave was closed to the public in 1963. Archaeologists discovered that the paintings were fading. They were fading because of all the visitors. Visitors breathed moisture into the cave. Mosses and green algae began to grow. This harmed the paintings, so officials closed the cave. A copy was made of the paintings and posted near the original cave. Now visitors can see a copy of what is inside Lascaux Cave.

15,000 years ago. The paintings are of wild animals such as horses, bulls, and bison.

Some historical writings and spoken stories can also help to locate sites. Some of these stories are actually legends. For example, the people of Tamil Nadu, South India, have a legend. They believe that they live atop what was once a beautiful, ancient city, and seven temples once stood where only one remains today. The legend states that the sea swallowed the other six temples and the ancient city. The people say that the gods ruined the city because they were jealous of its beauty.

According to *National Geographic*, two teams worked together to see if there was any truth to the legend. Marine archaeologists (archaeologists who study underwater sites) dove where local fishermen told them to dive. They found underwater ruins of an ancient civilization. The ruins and site spread for several miles.

Now the teams must study the site to see if it is related to the temple that still stands onshore. They will do underwater studies to find any signs that it was the legendary ancient city. It was possibly built more than 1,200 years ago.

Tricks of the Trade

Archaeologists use a number of methods to find sites. Methods can be as simple as walking on land and looking for clues. They can be as complex as using satellites that orbit Earth.

On Foot

Looking for a site on foot, or by looking at the land, is called a survey. Archaeologists walk while

History Told Him

Howard Carter was a famous archaeologist. His find was the tomb of an ancient Egyptian king named Tutankhamen. You may know him as King Tut.

Carter did not begin as an archaeologist. He was originally hired to draw pictures of finds in Egypt. He liked the excitement of excavations and discoveries. He decided to become an Egyptologist, or an archaeologist who studies ancient Egyptian cultures.

Carter was given permission to dig in an area known as the Valley of the Kings. Other archaeologists thought that the valley had been excavated as much as it could be. However,

Howard Carter *(holding box)* was a modern archaeologist who dug for science, not for riches or fame.

Carter found evidence that there would be another tomb there, that of King Tut. The evidence included written words about King Tut in the ancient temple of Karnak.

On November 4, 1922, Carter's team found the steps to the tomb. Over 3,500 artifacts were found. It took almost ten years to empty the tomb.

looking at details of the land. Some details will show that an archaeological site is there. For example, archaeologists look for differences in plant growth in an area. Differences in plant growth can show that a site may be beneath the ground. Plants grow taller over grave sites. Plants grow shorter when the soil is shallow. Shallow soil means that something solid is beneath, such as an ancient building. Metal detectors may also be used during a survey. The detectors can locate objects that have metal in them.

Early metal detectors, like this odd-shaped device being used in the English countryside, helped archaeologists discover possible dig sites. They often found primitive tools left over from human settlements.

Fast Fact

The ruins of the ancient city of Ubar in Oman were found in 1981 buried under sand. They were found by using radar images from satellites.

Using satellites is an extremely high-tech way to find sites. Satellites orbit Earth. They take photographs or images of land and sea. Archaeologists examine these photographs for certain features. The features show where a site may be. Photography from the sky is called aerial photography. Aerial photography can also be used to find sites underwater. Photographs of clear water can show outlines of sunken ships and ancient buildings.

Rough Seas

Weather and winds can create rough seas. Some underwater currents can stir up the seabed of archaeological sites. This can make it hard to see in the murky waters. Some archaeologists have found a way of working around rough seas.

Archaeologists built a special container at a site off the coast of Texas. The wreckage of a French ship from the 1700s had been found. The ship was named *La Belle*. The archaeologists built the container around the ship. It reached from the sea floor to the surface of the water. Ocean water was pumped out of the container. Archaeologists were able to excavate the site without being underwater.

Underwater

Underwater surveys also involve some high-tech machines. A survey may use a proton magnetometer. This machine is towed behind the survey vessel. It

searches for changes in Earth's magnetic field.
Changes in the field show that something iron or steel,
such as a ship, may be there. Metals such as iron and
steel cause changes in Earth's magnetic field.

Archaeologists can also use sonar technology.
Sonar technology sends sound waves toward the
seabed. The sound waves hit and bounce off the
seabed or objects that are there. This data is sent back
to a computer. The computer displays on a screen the
details of the seabed or any objects that are there.

Site Mapping and Excavation

An excavation changes a site. In truth, the excavation
actually ruins an archaeological site. Once a site has
been excavated, nothing remains in its original place.
Other archaeologists will not be able to study an
already excavated site.

What can be studied are the documents, maps, and
research details of an excavation. The archaeologist
must provide detailed information about the original
site. This way, archaeologists who were not present at a
dig can read about the dig many years later.

Correcting the Past

One dig can bring out thousands of artifacts. Mistakes are sometimes made in the process. Artifacts can be wrongly named or filed, and reports can contain errors as well.

Fortunately, there are many archaeologists who study reports and information from past digs. Some also search through and examine thousands of artifacts that are stored at museums and universities.

Ron Clarke and Phillip Tobias of Witwatersrand, Johannesburg, South Africa, found a mistake at a dig from such research. A drawer contained baboon fossils found at Sterkfontein (South Africa). Someone mistakenly put a cluster of bones in the drawer that were not from baboons. The bones actually belonged to a possible human ancestor. The cluster of bones, which were foot bones, belonged to a hominid. The hominid is an apelike creature. Clarke and Tobias named the bones Little Foot.

Maps are made of a site. An archaeologist can use a high-tech satellite system to get the map very exact. The global positioning system (GPS) works with satellites orbiting Earth. The satellites send down information to a hand-held device that receives the

Fast Fact

Loose clothes with many pockets are a favorite among archaeologists. Hiking boots are a no-go at sites. They are too big and clunky. Soft leather shoes with good treads are better for walking lightly in delicate areas.

information. The information tells the archaeologist exactly where he or she is. This makes location readings very exact.

Excavating a site changes it forever. Over the past thirty years, several sites around the world have been put together to resemble how they once looked. In this manner, the public can come and see how ancient people lived.

If time and money are not limited, the archaeologist can make very detailed maps and descriptions. He or she may use a total data station (TDS). This is a laser and computer system that maps the site very quickly and easily. Individual objects can be pinpointed on the map by using the laser.

Excavations are done in an orderly way. In many places the soil and rocks have layers. Soil and rocks get deposited over time, making layers. The top layers have formed most recently. As you dig deeper, you dig into layers that formed farther back in time. Artifacts are documented according to where and how they were found in each layer.

The excavation continues down through the layers. It stops when natural bedrock is reached. This is rock that is at the bottom of layers of deposited earth.

Archaeologists usually dig using a grid system. An area is measured and divided into squares. One square at a time is dug so that notes can be taken properly. The team may also do a block excavation. This is a dig that exposes large areas of soil at one time.

Archaeological Legacy

Artifacts are numbered, photographed, and drawn or described. Some are cleaned in a field laboratory that is set up near the site. Some artifacts are not cleaned. Ancient cutting tools are not cleaned so that they can be tested. Archaeologists look for deposits that may be left on the tools. This would include blood and fat from animals. By testing for deposits, archaeologists may learn what the tool was used for.

Artifacts that have been underwater or in moist soil for hundreds of thousands of years need very special care. Many of these artifacts will crumble once they are taken from the sea or any wet environment. If they are brought out, they are stored in water until they reach the lab.

Some delicate organic (natural) materials are freeze-dried. The object is first put into a wax liquid. Over time, the wax replaces any water in the object. This makes the object stronger. Then the object is freeze-dried. This takes out any remaining moisture.

Some artifacts will not be removed if the archaeologist feels that it is not safe to expose it to air. It may be because an object is too large or too fragile. These pieces will be documented, photographed, described, and left where they were found.

Learning from Artifacts

Archaeologists may also find human bones. How the bones are treated depends on where they are found. If descendants of the culture exist, they may request the bones for burial. If there are no remaining descendants, the bones may go to universities, museums, or local or state organizations.

An archaeologist who studies human bones is called an osteo-archaeologist. The osteo-archaeologist examines the human skeleton. He or she finds out how old the human was and if the person was male

Types of Finds

Archaeologists find many different types of artifacts:

- Bulk finds include building materials, stones, shells, and animal bones.
- Pottery is most often found broken. Grave sites may contain unbroken pottery. Pottery is a great find because it can be dated. Also, each culture used its own mixture to make pottery. By testing for what the pottery is made of, an archaeologist may learn which culture made it. For example, Romans were known to mix sand in their pottery mixtures.
- Small finds are less common objects made of different materials. Past humans have crafted or worked on them. They include:
  - Metal: jewelry, knives, coins
  - Bone: combs, pins
  - Stone: blades, arrowheads, daggers

or female. The archaeologist may also learn if the human was healthy or diseased.

Archaeologists may also experiment with modern materials. They try to make copies of the stone tools that they find. An archaeologist will chip at a stone as

42

Fast Fact

Studies of ancient human skulls from Peru show that ancient surgeries were performed. The skulls belonged to a civilization known as the Inca. The Inca cut holes into the skull. Surprisingly, the surgeries did not kill the patients. Archaeologists believe that the Inca did this to release evil spirits. The Inca may have believed that evil spirits caused headaches and mental problems.

Skeletons can tell archaeologists how a person might have died. Scratches across the ribs or neck bones may suggest the person was stabbed or cut. Some scratches might indicate ancient surgery!

Historic Specialty

Some archaeologists study past cultures that have written records. These records could be diaries, government papers, letters, drawings, photographs, or maps.

Many historic written accounts do not include details about the lives of common people. Historical archaeologists try to find out details about common life in historic cultures. They examine any artifacts of that time including clothing, tools, and furniture.

Some historic sites that no longer stand are rebuilt. Architects and historians use the help of archaeologists to do so. Historical archaeologists research details at or about the original site. They provide information so that the copies are as close to the originals as possible.

he or she believes a past culture did. Chipping stone to make a tool is called flintknapping. It also helps archaeologists to understand broken artifacts and stones found at a site.

Archaeologists also examine the physical features of a site. If they find foundations of early houses or dwellings, they examine the design and size. They can learn how many people may have lived in one building. A culture may have burned wood for cooking food. The wood becomes charcoal. Charcoal may be found at a site. The charcoal can be tested for its date of origin.

Archaeologists may find other objects at a site that were not made by humans. These are called ecofacts. An ecofact is an organic or natural object from the past. An ecofact could be a preserved grain seed or bits of pollen. Ecofacts are tested to see what they are. They can tell an archaeologist what types of plants existed during the culture's time.

Where It All Comes Together

Artifacts are usually stored in museums and universities. Museums may put the artifacts on display or store them for archaeological research. Artifacts may also be sent to university labs and hospital labs for testing. The archaeologist may also continue to study the artifacts once they are in the museums or universities.

The archaeologist brings together all the information of the excavation in a report. The report states

Archaeological finds feed the imaginations of students all over the world. A fascination with skeletons and life in the ancient world can lead young people to begin lives as archaeologists, anthropologists, or paleontologists.

what was done and why it was done. It states what the archaeologist or the archaeological team discovered. If the archaeologist's goal was to discover a culture and all its details, then he or she explains this in his or her report. Photographs, maps, drawings, and field information provide many details for the report. This process can take months and even years to finish.

Kids in Action

Some lucky students took part in an excavation of a 70-million-year-old dinosaur in Wyoming. The excavation was part of Project Exploration. The students were able to dig, learn about desert wildlife, and explore local ranches.

Project Exploration is run by paleontologist Paul Sereno and his wife, Gabrielle Lyon. Paleontologists study fossils. Project Exploration gives children a first-hand view of excavation work and ancient study.

Sereno has made several important discoveries throughout his career. He was part of a team that discovered the bones of a 110-million-year-old giant crocodile. It is named *Sarcosuchus imperator*, which means "flesh crocodile emperor." Sereno nicknamed it "the Super Croc." It was as long as a city bus and weighed almost 9 tons (17,500 pounds, or

7,938 kilograms). Its weight can be compared to that of a small whale. Its jaws were almost 6 feet (1.8 meters) long. It was found at Gadoufaoua in Niger, Africa.

Places to Work

Archaeologists work in three main areas: colleges or universities, museums and foundations, and for private companies or the government. Salaries range from $16,000 to more than $50,000 a year.

- Archaeologists who work in academic areas teach. Many do research and publish their findings.
- Archaeologists who work for museums may preserve and repair ancient objects. They may also do research and publish their findings. Many work to educate the public about a museum's artifacts.
- Archaeologists who work for the government and private companies work in cultural resource management. They work to save sites from ruin by construction projects and disasters. They may educate the public about projects.

If You Dig It

To be an archaeologist you must get a college education. After college, most archaeologists continue on to get a master's degree. At this point, many archaeologists will declare an area of specialty. For example, an archaeologist may decide that he or she will become an expert in the Mayan civilization.

Fortunately, the public can get involved in archaeology without having a background in it. Local museums may offer programs for students interested in archaeology. Each state has an archaeological organization. Many local organizations sponsor digs where young people can participate. Some states offer junior archaeology clubs and activities. You can ask your teacher or librarian to help you find your state or local archaeological clubs and organizations. You can also find some resources in the back of this book.

Some government agencies may also offer local participation. These agencies include local units of the Forest Service and the National Park Service. Other local units may include the Bureau of Land Management, the Bureau of Reclamation, and the Army Corps of Engineers.

Local universities may allow field trips and visits to the archaeological department. You can also visit the Web sites of the organizations listed at the back of this book. Happy digging!

Glossary

aerial photography Photographs taken of land and sea from the sky or space.

anthropology The study of human beings, past and present.

archaeological site Any place that has evidence of past human life.

archaeology The study of past human life.

artifact An object that was made, changed, or used by humans.

block excavation A dig that exposes large areas of soil at a time.

chart To make a map or drawing that shows information.

civilization An organized society.

cultural resource management The survey, possible excavation, and protection of sites.

culture A group of people who live in the same way with the same values, customs, and beliefs.

ecofact An organic or natural object from the past.

examine To look carefully at something.

excavate To dig out from the earth.

extinct A type of living thing that has died out.

find A valuable or important discovery.

flintknapping Chipping stone to make a tool.

grid system A set of straight lines that cross each other to make squares.

midden Trash deposits from the past.

organic Natural, having to do with or coming from living things.

prehistoric Time before the written word was used.

preserved Something that lasts in its original state.

primate Any member of a group of intelligent mammals that includes humans, apes, and monkeys.

proton magnetometer A machine that finds changes in Earth's magnetic field.

sonar technology A technique where sound waves are sent out and measured when they hit an object and bounce back.

unearth To dig something up.

For More Information

Organizations

Archaeological Institute of America (AIA)
   at Boston University
656 Beacon Street
Boston, MA 02215-2006
(617) 353-6550
Web site: http://www.archaeological.org

Center for American Archeology
Kampsville Archeological Center
P.O. Box 366
Kampsville, IL 62053
(618) 653-4316
Web site: http://www.caa-archeology.org

Crow Canyon Archaeological Center
23390 County Road K
Cortez, CO 81321-9909
(800) 422-8975
Web site: http://www.crowcanyon.org

Institute of Nautical Archaeology
P.O. Drawer HG
College Station, TX 77841-5137
(979) 845-6694
Web site: http://ina.tamu.edu

National Park Service
Archaeological Division
Publication Coordinator
P.O. Box 37127
Washington, DC 20013-7127
Web site: http://www.nps.gov

National Trust for Historic Preservation
1785 Massachusetts Avenue NW
Washington, DC 20036
Web site: http://www.nthp.org

Society for American Archaeology
900 Second Street NE, Suite 12
Washington, DC 20002-3557
(202) 789-8200
Web site: http://www.saa.org

Society for Historical Archaeology
P.O. Box 30446
Tucson, AZ 85751-0446
Web site: http://www.sha.org

Web sites

Due to the changing nature of Internet links, the Rosen Publishing Group, Inc., has developed an online list of Web sites related to the subject of this book. This site is updated regularly. Please use this link to access the list:

http://www.rosenlinks.com/ec/arch

For Further Reading

Cranfield, Ingrid. *The Archaeology Kit: Science Action Book*. Philadelphia: Running Press, 1998.

Laubenstein, Karen, and Ron Roy. *Archaeology Smart Junior: Discovering History's Buried Treasures*. New York: Princeton Review, 1997.

McGowen, Tom. *Adventures in Archaeology* (Scientific American Sourcebooks). Breckenridge, CO: Twenty-First Century Books, 1997.

Panchyk, Richard. *Archaeology for Kids: Uncovering the Mysteries of Our Past*. Chicago: Chicago Review Press, 2001.

Rees, Rosemary. *The Ancient Greeks* (Understanding People in the Past). Portsmouth, NH: Heinemann Library, 2001.

Shuter, Jane. *Ancient Egypt* (History Beneath Your

Feet). New York: Raintree/Steck Vaughn, 2000.

Smith, KC. *Ancient Shipwrecks* (Watts Library: Shipwrecks). Danbury, CT: Franklin Watts, 2000.

Bibliography

Ashmore, Wendy, and Robert J. Sharer. *Discovering Our Past: A Brief Introduction to Archaeology.* Third edition. Columbus, OH: McGraw-Hill, 1999.

Block, Ira. "Inca Rescue—Field Notes from Photographer Ira Block." Retrieved 2002 (http://magma.nationalgeographic.com/ngm/0205/feature5/assignment2.html).

Canterbury Archaeological Trust Limited. "Archaeology, Past and Present." Retrieved August 2002 (http://www.canterburytrust.co.uk/schools/discover/discov01.htm).

Carrell, Toni L. "Underwater News." *SHA Newsletter.* Retrieved August 2002 (http://www.sha.org/CurrRes/nlcruw.htm).

Cock, Guillermo A. "Inca Rescue." Retrieved August

2002 (http://magma.nationalgeographic.com/ngm/0205/feature5/index.html).

Crabtree, Pam J., and Douglas V. Campana. *Archaeology and Prehistory*. Columbus, OH: McGraw-Hill Higher Education, 2001.

Gore, Rick. "The Dawn of Humans—Expanding Worlds." *National Geographic*. May 1997, pp. 85–109.

Gore, Rick. "The Dawn of Humans—The First Steps." *National Geographic*. February 1997, pp. 72–99.

Gore, Rick. "The Dawn of Humans—Neanderthals?" *National Geographic*. January 1996, pp. 2–35.

Handwerk, Brian. "New Underwater Finds Raise Questions About Flood Myths." *National Geographic News*. May 28, 2002. Retrieved August 2002 (http://news.nationalgeographic.com/news/2002/05/0528_020528_sunkencities.html).

Handwerk, Brian "Pyramid Builders' Village Found in Egypt." *National Geographic News*. August 5, 2002. Retrieved August 2002 (http://news.nationalgeographic.com/news/2002/08/0805_020805_giza.html).

Hester, Thomas R. "Archaeology." World Book Online Americas Edition. Retrieved August 2002 (http://www.worldbookonline.com/ar?/na/ar/co/ar028320.htm).

Hester, Thomas R., Kenneth L. Feder, and Harry J. Shafer. *Field Methods in Archaeology*. Columbus, OH: Mayfield Publishing Company, 1997.

National Geographic Society. "Archaeology: Finding, Dating, and Interpreting Objects." 2002. Retrieved August 2002 (http://www.nationalgeographic.com:80/eye/archaeology/effect.html).

National Geographic Society. "Inca Mummies—Secrets of a Lost World." 2002. Retrieved August 2002 (http://www.nationalgeographic.com/inca/).

Parsell, D. L. "Skull Fossil Opens Window into Early Period of Human Origins." *National Geographic News*. July 11, 2002. Retrieved August 2002 (http://news.nationalgeographic.com/news/2002/07/0710_020710_chadskull.html).

Parsell, D. L. "'SuperCroc' Fossil Found in Sahara." *National Geographic News*. October 25, 2001. Retrieved August 2002. (http://news.nationalgeographic.com/news/2001/10/1025_supercroc.html).

The Society for Historical Archaeology. "Is the Past in

Your Future?" Retrieved August 2002
(http://www.sha.org/sha_kbro.htm).
Spry, Marla J., Ashley Dumas, and Wes Shaw.
"What Is Archaeology?" Retrieved August 2002
(http://bama.ua.edu/~alaarch/
what_is_archaeology_/what_is_archaeology_.html).

Index

About the Author

Holly Cefry is a freelance writer. Her books have been placed on the Voice of Youth Advocates National Nonfiction Honor List. She is a member of the Authors Guild and the Society for Children's Book Writers and Illustrators.

Photo Credits

Designer: Les Kanturek; Editor: Mark Beyer; Layout: Thomas Forget